BRITAIN IN OLD PH(

C000297858

Darlaston, Moxley & Bentley

IAN M. BOTT

Lt Whitehead

OWNER

SUTTON PUBLISHING LIMITED

Sutton Publishing Limited
Phoenix Mill · Thrupp · Stroud
Gloucestershire · GL5 2BU

First published 2000

Title page photograph: W. Martin Winn
employees don sailors' uniforms for this
patriotic parade of the mid-1930s (see also
page 85). The company, which produced
nuts and bolts, was situated in Kendricks
Road. (David Robinson)

British Library Cataloguing in Publication Data
A catalogue record for this book is available from the
British Library.

ISBN 0-7509-2533-7

Typeset in 10.5/13.5 Photina.
Typesetting and origination by
Sutton Publishing Limited.
Printed and bound in England by
J.H. Haynes & Co. Ltd, Sparkford.

THE BLACK COUNTRY SOCIETY

This voluntary society, affiliated to the Civic Trust, was founded
in 1967 as a reaction to the trend of the late 1950s and early
1960s to amalgamate everything into large units and in the
Midlands to sweep away the area's industrial heritage in the
process.

The general aim of the Society is to create interest in the past, present and future of
the Black Country, and early on it campaigned for the establishment of an industrial
museum. In 1975 the Black Country Living Museum was started by Dudley Borough
Council on 26 acres of totally derelict land adjoining the grounds of Dudley Castle. This
has developed into an award-winning museum which attracts over 250,000 visitors
annually.

It was announced in August 1998 that having secured a lottery grant of nearly £3
million, the Museum Board will be able to authorize the start of work on a £4.5 million
state-of-the-art interpretation centre. This will be known as the 'Rolfe Street Project',
named after the street which once housed the Smethwick Baths. The façade of this
Victorian building is to be incorporated into the new interpretation centre.

At the Black Country Living Museum there is a boat dock fully equipped to restore
narrowboats of wood and iron and different vessels can be seen on the dock throughout
the year. From behind the Bottle and Glass Inn visitors can travel on a canal boat into
Dudley Canal Tunnel, a memorable journey to see spectacular limestone caverns and the
fascinating Castle Mill Basin.

There are 2,500 members of the Black Country Society and all receive the quarterly
magazine *The Blackcountryman*, of which 124 issues have been published since its
founding in 1967. In the whole collection there are some 1,800 authoritative articles on
all aspects of the Black Country by historians, teachers, researchers, students, subject
experts and ordinary folk with an extraordinary story to tell. The whole constitutes a
unique resource about the area and is a mine of information for students and researchers
who frequently refer to it. Many schools and libraries are subscribers. Three thousand
copies of the magazine are printed each quarter. It is non-commercial, and contributors
do not receive payment for their articles.

PO Box 71 · Kingswinford · West Midlands DY6 9YN

CONTENTS

Burns Road, Moxley, is part of a large post-war housing estate to the east of the High Street. The actual address of the shops and flats on the right is Roberts Close. (Jean Phillips)

Darlaston's parish church of St Lawrence pictured in 1871. The following year the brick factory-like nave was rebuilt in stone to complement the tower of 1606. Many ancient graves were disturbed in 1873 when the burial ground wall was relocated to widen the surrounding highways of Church Street and New Street. (Author)

INTRODUCTION

Close examination of pre-1974 maps of Staffordshire reveals that once there were two settlements called Darlaston in that county. One – near Stone – still retains its original status, while the other – near Walsall and the subject of this book – has been part of the West Midlands for the last twenty-six years. Together with neighbours Moxley and Bentley, the town became the administrative centre of Darlaston Urban District Council, formed in 1894, with its town hall and council chamber prematurely dating from 1888. The outlying district of Kings Hill has also been incorporated into these pages, sharing Darlaston, Moxley and Bentley's fate of being amalgamated with larger neighbour Walsall Council in 1966.

The absence of Darlaston from the Domesday Book suggests that it was established in the years following the Norman Conquest with the original spelling of 'Deorlaveston', meaning 'the place of Deorlav'. The parish church of St Lawrence, however, is mentioned in 1406 but is believed to have been founded in the twelfth century by the first lord of the manor, William de Darlastonia. The parish registers date from 1539.

In his book *The History and Antiquities of Staffordshire, Volume Two*, published in 1801, the Revd Stebbing Shaw informs us that Darlaston comprised 800 acres, 30 of which were given over to meadow, the rest being fields of wheat, barley and oats. Of interest, he mentions ancient wells 10 yards deep to the north of the church and one 25 yards deep to the south. Important, though, is his observation of several coal pits, ironstone workings and the availability of brick, tile and quarry clay. Like the rest of the Black Country, Darlaston was set to change forever from a rural to an industrial landscape, playing its part in the great Industrial Revolution.

Early industries included the production of nails, buckles, chapes and stirrups, but the town was more famous in the seventeenth and eighteenth centuries for the manufacture of gun locks – the firing mechanism of a gun. At nearby Wednesbury gun barrels were produced and both towns became wealthy from supplying weapons to the Napoleonic Wars (1804–15). In modern times, though, Darlaston became the leading manufacturing base in the world of the humble nut and bolt. Many of the town's streets have been named after the pioneers of this industry over the last 130 years or so, such as Richards, Wiley and Garrington. The largest manufacturer was Guest, Keen and Nettlefold's (GKN), which bought out many smaller firms and was based at the huge Atlas Works. Two names quintessentially Darlaston are Rubery and Owen. John Tunner Rubery formed a business partnership in 1893 with Alfred Ernest Owen, an engineer from Wrexham, together establishing what was to become the Rubery Owen organisation, which still has interests in the town today.

Moxley too has long been a centre of industry with ironworks lining the route of the Walsall Canal of 1799, which passes through the village, and in former times coalmining and the extraction of sand and clay. Until recently clay pots and ropes were produced here.

An astonishing drama unfolded here on 10 August 1813 at the Moorcroft Colliery belonging to Messrs Scott and Foley, joint lords of the manor. Following a sudden crowning in (a vent in the mine workings), eight men and a boy aged twelve found themselves trapped underground, cut off from the mineshaft by tons of debris which killed two men and a horse in its fall. With word soon getting around, thousands of spectators converged on the spot, many forming teams who – relieving one another – worked around the clock to sink a rescue shaft to the confined miners. Straw faggots were used to help prevent the sandy subsoil from filling the emergency excavation. Soon desperate tappings could be heard from the subterranean prison, encouraging the already exhausted rescuers to work on at speed. Finally, after seven days, the victims were reached and gruel was passed to them through the carefully opened cavity, so as to allow them to recover some strength whilst protecting the already dangerous environment from a violent rush of air. When they were brought to the surface, it is said that one woman relative died of 'excess of joy'. All victims survived.

Bentley is today a dormitory for Darlaston with much of its housing stock being post-Second World War. Indeed, many of its streets are named after British war heroes. Bentley Hall was the setting in September 1651 for one of the instalments in the escape of Charles II from Parliamentarian persecution following defeat at the battle of Worcester (see page 52). In recent years the old Darlaston Urban District has been physically chopped in two with the opening of the keyway, a dual carriageway in a deep cutting, linking up with junction 10 of the M6 between Darlaston and Bentley.

The main entrance to the Bentley housing estate, Queen Elizabeth Avenue, *c.* 1966. The sign has now gone and the grass pedestrian refuge is replaced by concrete. Trees grow today on the bare mound topped by Emmanuel church, once the site of Bentley Hall. (Stan Hill)

1

Darlaston Town Centre

The Bull Stake from John Wootton House multi-storey flats, 1966. Once the site of the barbaric pastime of bull baiting, this busy crossroads has long been the focal point of Darlaston town centre. In the foreground King Street emerges from the left to meet Pinfold Street from the right. The bus has just turned out of Darlaston Road into Walsall Road. (Darlaston Rotary Club)

Horse-drawn traffic emerges from King Street into the Bull Stake in this very rare picture of about 1890. (Author)

Here the Bull Stake is viewed from Pinfold Street, showing King Street to the left and Walsall Road to the right, *c.* 1900. The large corner house was later to become a branch of the Wednesbury Building Society (see page 15). (Black Country Living Museum)

Passengers board a single-deck electric tram outside the Old Castle hotel, *c.* 1910. To the right is parked a delivery van from the Park Laundry. Another old Darlaston hostelry, visible in the centre of the picture, is the Waggon and Horses, King Street. (National Tramway Museum)

The Waggon and Horses, King Street, seen here in about 1905, was one of Darlaston's oldest inns. The name of the licensee displayed above the entrance is William G. France. (Author)

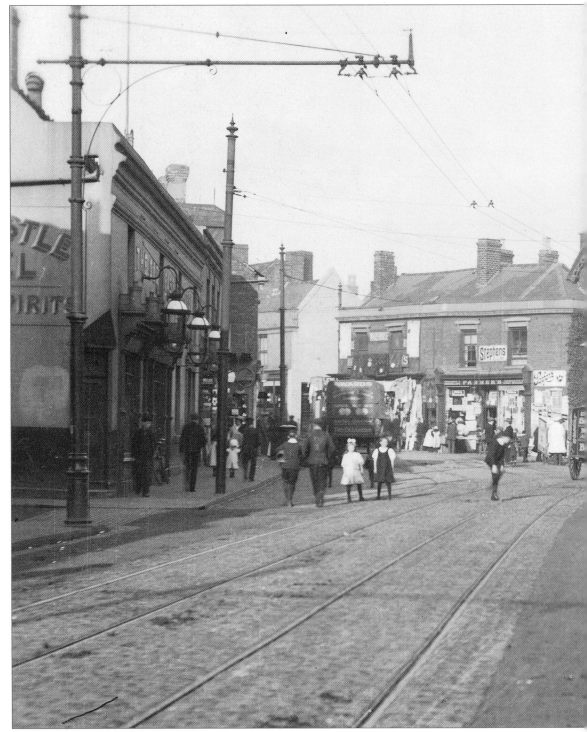

Looking along Pinfold Street towards the Bull Stake, *c.* 1910. In the centre of the picture a horse-drawn delivery van advertises 'Smart's noted bread'. (Author)

This view of the Bull Stake is taken from Walsall Road, showing to the left its junction with Darlaston Road, *c.* 1912. The premises of Hobson's ironmongers is today occupied by OBC insurance brokers. (Terry Price)

Hobson's ironmongers appears to the right of this picture, looking in the opposite direction to that above, *c.* 1910. Walsall Road, as the name suggests, was the main route to Darlaston's larger neighbour. The boy to the left carries a hoop, which was a favourite childhood amusement of this era. The clock visible on the tram pole-cum-lamp standard, informs us that it was half past one in the afternoon. (Terry Price)

Opening day for the Darlaston branch of Wednesbury Building Society was 29 July 1954; potential savers gather around the Bull Stake premises. Note the tannoy mounted above the entrance porch. (Olive Swift)

Trams had disappeared from Darlaston's streets by 1940 and were later superseded by the trolleybus. Here a route no. 2 trolleybus negotiates the Bull Stake traffic island, 9 November 1961. This was the terminus of a journey from Whitmore Reans in Wolverhampton. In turn, trolleybuses vanished from Darlaston on 8 August 1965. (The late J.C. Brown)

A view across Bull Stake traffic island towards Pinfold Street, 7 September 1968. To the right of the Old Castle Hotel are David Jones and Son, corn dealer, and T.W. Baker who, unexpectedly, was a butcher. (Alan Price)

Another view along Pinfold Street, showing the Three Horseshoes public house to the left, 1950s. (Author)

Passengers alight from a trolleybus near Pinfold Street Methodist chapel, 10 August 1964. On the opposite carriageway a stationary service vehicle warns 'danger – overhead repairs'. (The late J.C. Brown)

Three horseshoes visible on the parapet of the white-painted public house confirm its name and location along Pinfold Street, 7 September 1968. Pinfold Street and its continuation, Moxley Road, link Darlaston to Moxley. (Alan Price)

The trolleybus which served routes 2 and 7 is now heading back along Pinfold Street at the start of its journey to Wolverhampton, 26 August 1964. Amongst the businesses is Len Mitchell's Cycles Ltd. (The late J.C. Brown)

Len Mitchell moved his cycle business from Kings Hill (see page 93) to 8 Pinfold Street in 1934, which had previously traded as Sid Frost Cycles. Len – pictured at the shop entrance – retired in 1963 and the business was carried on by family and loyal staff, expanding into neighbouring properties until closure in 1982. (Marion Evans)

King Street, seen here in the 1950s from the Bull Stake, is Darlaston's main shopping street, once abundant with long-established family businesses. Nos 1–2 King Street, Appleyard's drapers, is now the site of the modern Darlaston library, opened 5 August 1987. (Black Country Living Museum)

The same view as above, 1960. At the centre of the traffic island stands a lamp which originally burnt off sewer gases. The island was replaced by traffic lights in 1977. (Black Country Living Museum)

King Street, mid-1920s. The gentle gradient climbs to meet Church Street, the highest ground in an otherwise flat landscape. (National Tramway Museum)

This 1966 view of King Street shows clearly the buildings on the left-hand side of the road, all of which have now been demolished. When the last original building – Phillips' chemist – was torn down in January 1988, it was found to be of a seventeenth-century timber-framed construction. (Darlaston Rotary Club)

King Street, again in 1966, this time on a rainy day. Kingston's the butcher is one of the original buildings that survive today as far as the tall three-storey buildings centre right. (Bernard Minton)

The doorway in the left foreground marks King Street's junction with the High Street. This was the entrance to John Adey's butcher's shop. Victoria House, top right, was once Darlaston's post office. Further beyond in this 1966 picture can be seen the junction with Church Street. (Bernard Minton)

King Street from the direction of Church Street, 1956. Victoria House is seen again, to the right of Valeting Service. These premises survive, whilst all the properties on the right-hand side have been demolished – including the three-storey white-painted Dog and Partridge public house. (Author)

The White Lion public house, situated in The Fold, just off King Street is pictured dressed up for the coronation of Queen Elizabeth II, 2 June 1953. Until the completion of the town hall in 1888 this was the venue for meetings of the Local Board, which governed Darlaston until 1894. A magistrate's court was also held here. The 'Wednesbury Mob' are said to have rested here when conveying the Revd John Wesley to Bentley Hall during the Wednesbury anti-Methodist riot on 20 October 1743. For many years the White Lion was kept by Charles and Sally Nicholls, the paternal grandparents of the actress Sue Nicholls, fondly known as Audrey Roberts in Coronation Street (see page 79). (Black Country Living Museum)

Victoria Road, seen here in about 1930, was originally called Pardoe's Lane, but renamed in honour of Queen Victoria's golden jubilee in 1887. Also in that year the foundation stone of the town hall was laid. This building – on the left – opened on 31 October 1888. In the centre can be seen the White Lion, situated in The Fold. To the right are the old St Lawrence's rectory (now demolished) and the post office dating from 1912. (Author)

This view of Victoria Road was taken at the junction of Church Street, left and King Street, right, looking towards Bull Piece, *c*. 1910. The high boundary wall to the left enclosed the gardens of St Lawrence's rectory. A man on horseback passes the town hall at the centre of the picture. The building with the large lamp is the Swan Hotel, which still survives along with all the shops pictured. (Author)

Another view of Victoria Road, this time from Victoria Park, 1909. St Lawrence's rectory can be seen on the far left, whilst St Lawrence's church dominates the town centre. Immediately to the left of the church can be seen the dovecote which once belonged to Darlaston House, the former home of Samuel Mills, ironmaster. To the right are the houses in Rectory Avenue, built on the site of Darlaston House. The single-storey building was opened in 1901 as the Girls' Institute, the gift of Miss Jane Mills. (Author)

Peace celebrations were held at the town hall in 1919 following the end of the First World War. Designed by Jethro Cossins of Birmingham and built by Thomas Tildesley, the town hall also housed a library and was the venue for many recitals and wedding receptions. (Author)

The Picturedrome is shown newly built in 1911. Situated in Crescent Road, this ornate cinema with its Palladian lantern was closed to the public in 1956 and eventually demolished in 1963. (Eric Woolley)

Bounded by Victoria Road and Crescent Road, Victoria Park was opened in 1903. In the distance to the left can be seen the police station of 1899 and the town hall to the right. (Author)

The bandstand, Victoria Park, 1931. Darlaston once possessed three bandstands, the others being in George Rose Park (see page 120) and Kings Hill Park (see page 94). (Author)

High Street, 1966, by which time much demolition had already taken place. Originally named Cock Street, it was of a lesser importance than King Street for shopping. At the head of the road can be seen Burton's tailors in King Street. High Street was swept away in the 1970s, to be replaced by a pedestrian square and a now empty superstore. (Bernard Minton)

Darlaston carnival parade makes its way through Church Street, mid-1970s. The gentleman wearing spectacles in the foreground is the late Malcolm Timmins, Darlaston historian. (Marjorie Stockham)

2

Moxley

Moxley grew as a community of ironworkers and miners at the meeting of three main roads, from Bilston, Wednesbury and Darlaston. It was formed as an ecclesiastical parish on 8 July 1845. This 1950 view is of Church Street as it merges into High Street. Near the telephone box to the left a delivery is being made to Page's butchers. The white-painted building on the right was the Old Britannia public house. Sadly, everything visible in the picture has now been swept away. (Author)

The spire of All Saints' church can just be discerned in this 1950s view of the High Street. The low wall, in the centre of the left-hand buildings, marks the position of Bourne Primitive Methodist chapel. (All Saints' Church)

This view of High Street was taken from the junction of Burns Road, right, looking towards Bilston, 1950s. The Wesleyan Sunday school has now gone – along with all the houses to the left, whilst the petrol pumps have disappeared from the right. (All Saints' Church)

A trolleybus makes its way along High Street passing the Wesleyan chapel and adjoining Sunday school, 16 November 1963. The cyclist laden with shopping is probably making her way home from the Burns Road stores. (The late J.C. Brown)

Built in 1853, the Wesleyan chapel in the High Street is seen here in about 1900. Today the old chapel and Sunday school have been replaced by a modern Wesleyan centre. (Jean Phillips)

High Street, looking towards Bilston, 2 July 1962. To the right can be seen Bourne Primitive Methodist chapel, which was erected in 1873. The shop to the left of the chapel is today a Chinese take-away. (The late J.C. Brown)

The congregation of Bourne chapel pose for the camera, 1953. The minister, Mr Brown, can be seen in the pulpit on the right. (Cynthia Wilkes)

Bourne officials line up for this picture taken in 1950. Left to right: Cynthia Wilkes, Marjorie Lewis, Les Bagby, Mr Hinton, Mr Pooler, Mr Fellows, Arthur Felton, Ike Morris, Mrs Felton, Mrs Fellows, Charlie Moore, Bill Mills, Gladys Bailey, Christopher Lloyd. (Cynthia Wilkes)

The limestone war memorial is blessed before a well-turned-out crowd of Moxley villagers. Sited at the junction of Church Street and Moxley Road, the memorial is inscribed 'AMDG. In memory of the men from this parish who fell in the Great War 1914–18'. (Horace Page)

Looking along Moxley Road towards Darlaston, with the Swan Inn far left, *c.* 1955. To the right is the war memorial behind which can be seen All Saints' church. With the exception of the memorial and church, everything else has been removed and replaced by a giant multi-lane traffic island. (All Saints' Church)

Two trolleybuses pass along Moxley Road, 15 May 1964. These 'whispering giants' were an environmentally friendly bus service powered from an overhead electric cable. (The late J.C. Brown)

Moxley hospital was developed on the site of the former Moorcroft colliery, reached by a lengthy carriage drive from Bull Lane. Firstly administered by the South Staffordshire Joint Smallpox Hospital Board, it was later operated by the West Bromwich and District Hospitals Management Committee. Members of the Salvation Army are seen arriving on Easter Sunday in the 1950s carrying baskets of hard boiled eggs. (Author)

The Salvation Army band strikes up watched by a nurse and some young patients. In 1900 the President of the Royal Society, Sir Oliver Lodge, instigated the re-afforestation of the surrounding colliery waste with saplings from the Royal Sandringham estates. This is known today as Moorcroft Wood. Moxley Hospital was pulled down in the 1990s and today the site is occupied by the Hawkswood Grange housing development. (Author)

Standing in Church Street, part of Thomas Telford's London to Holyhead road, All Saints' parish church was erected in 1851 on a plot of land previously known as Little Moxley Field. The octagonal broach spire was added in 1877 by Thomas and Charles Wells of Eaton Mascott Hall, Shropshire, in memory of their father, Thomas senior. Pictured here in 1950, the properties to the left of the church have long been demolished. (Jean Phillips)

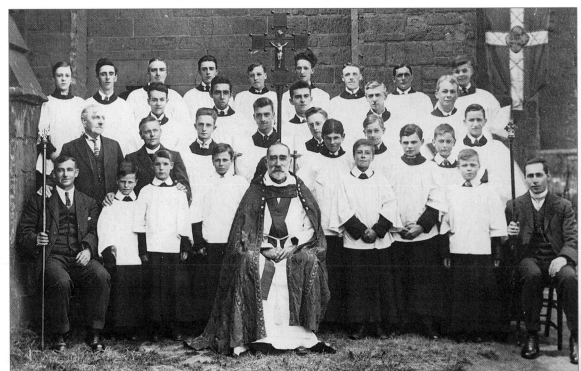

The Revd Mr Benson is pictured with All Saints' male choir, c. 1924. (All Saints' Church)

A working party of parishioners is pictured giving All Saints' interior a coat of paint in 1955. The photograph has obviously been very carefully staged. (All Saints' Church)

Work done, the paint-spattered party re-assembles for a final picture. (All Saints' Church)

Parishioners assemble outside All Saints' vicarage, 1965. Back row, left to right: Jack Dyke, Lena Nash, Bill Nash, Minnie Kirk, Kath Warner, Maria Mills, Floss Low, -?-, -?-, Mrs Thacker (with baby), the Revd Kenneth Thacker, Jess Wood, -?-, Jack Mills, David Slater. Front row: Ellen Dyke, Rose Wood, Jean Mills, Gwen Sedgwick, -?-. Built in 1859, the vicarage is today named Poplar House and has been converted to flats. (Gwen Sedgwick)

An All Saints' church parade passes the war memorial in 1962. Foreground, left to right: -?-, Joe Lowe, the Revd Peter Heselton. (All Saints' Church)

A Bedford lorry from the fleet of William Wesson's Victoria ironworks is turned into a mobile classroom for an All Saints' Sunday school festival in 1963. Wesson's were founded as Wright and Wesson in 1898 on a site in Bull Lane. (All Saints' Church)

Before motorised power was introduced Wesson's products were dispatched on horse-drawn drays. The stables were located to the rear of the Wesson family home, The Heath, situated opposite the Moxley end of Bull Lane. Harry Page senior is pictured between the right-hand pair of horses in about 1920. (Horace Page)

William Wesson's home, The Heath, can be seen to the left, viewed across flooded excavations where sand was extracted. A whole street of houses named Heath Acres now occupies the site of the house and gardens. The photograph, taken in about 1940, also shows housing along Holyhead Road, a continuation of Church Street. (Horace Page)

Wesleyan Methodist choristers gather in the garden of The Heath, *c.* 1905. With no public park in Moxley, Mr Wesson's garden made an acceptable pleasure ground. (Valerie Allen)

William Henry Wesson (1874–1936), who resided at The Heath and was owner of the Victoria ironworks. When he was ill with pneumonia, peat was spread on the main road outside The Heath to muffle the sound of passing traffic. (Horace Page)

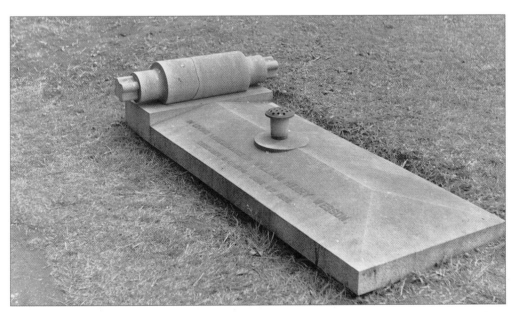

William Henry Wesson's grave in All Saints' churchyard is unique, as the headstone is in the form of a roller used in a steel rolling mill. Here it is in about 1965. (Bernard Minton)

An all-male party of Wesson's workers are seen enjoying a charabanc outing to Matlock, Derbyshire, 1924. (Horace Page)

Another outing from Wesson's, this time a day trip to Southport made up of retired staff, *c.* 1938. (Horace Page)

Wesson's employees enjoying a dinner party, *c.* 1949. Although the company is now part of a large conglomerate, the Wesson name is still used today. (Horace Page)

Hand-throwing a plant pot at George Ward (Moxley) Limited at Baggotts Bridge, 1966. Approached from Heathfield Lane West, Darlaston, the site was first used for the production of bricks. When the better quality clay was exhausted, it was found that the remainder made porous bricks, therefore production was cleverly switched to the manufacture of plant pots. (Darlaston Rotary Club)

In this delightful study from 1933, Moxley youngster Horace Page takes to the wheel of his plywood constructed pedal car. (Horace Page)

1st Moxley scouts are pictured following a successful jamboree, with the winners' cup, *c.* 1930. (Horace Page)

The safe return of sailor Billy Bagby from service in the Second World War is celebrated on land off Moxley Road. Hero Billy, seated at the head of the table, wears his seaman's uniform. (Valerie Allen)

Moxley Wesleyans FC obviously had a very successful 1923/4 season judging by their shield and victory cup. (David Phillips)

Local children and their guardians on the forecourt of the Red Lion public house, Moxley Road, 1950. (Author)

Tommy Upton drinks from a large earthenware vessel assisted by Joe Ward, watched by fellow regulars of the George Inn, Church Street, during a summer outing. (Jim Oakley)

Rival tug-of-war teams battle it out at the Wilkinson Road coronation celebrations, 2 June 1953. (Horace Page)

Wilkinson Road youngsters enjoy the goodies laid on for the coronation street party. (Horace Page)

Old Moxley. These Queen Street properties were swept away during slum clearance programmes carried out in 1934. Spacious parlour-type houses took their place. (Sam Stevenson)

New Moxley. Roberts Close shops, *c.* 1960. Original traders included John Smith, chemist, and Foster's drapery store. (Stan Hill)

3

Bentley

Bentley is today a residential suburb, part of which was transferred to Darlaston Urban District in 1934. This belies its origins as an ancient rural manor once owned by the Earls of Lichfield. Bentley Hall, one-time home of the Lane family, is pictured here in 1906. This was an eighteenth-century building on the site of the original house. (Author)

This nineteenth-century engraving depicts the original Bentley Hall as King Charles II would have known it. The desperate royal arrived at Bentley – the home of Colonel John Lane – late in the evening of Tuesday 9 September 1651, following disastrous defeat at the hands of the Parliamentarians in the Battle of Worcester. During the previous five days sanctuary had been provided at White Ladies Priory and Boscobel House in Shropshire and also at Moseley Old Hall in Staffordshire. At this time England had already experienced nine years of civil war. In 1649 Charles I had been beheaded at Whitehall and the country declared a Commonwealth headed by Oliver Cromwell, the Lord Protector. The then Prince Charles left England for France, later residing in Holland. From there he sailed to Scotland, where he was crowned Charles II on 1 January 1651. Now there was a price on his head too.

The King had been escorted from Moseley to Bentley by Colonel Lane himself as part of a pre-arranged escape plan. In the early hours of the following morning Charles set off on horseback, accompanied by the colonel's sister, Lady Jane Lane, on a journey to Trent, near Yeovil in Somerset, the King disguised as her manservant, William Jackson. After parting company at Trent, Lady Jane returned to Bentley whilst the King continued to the coast at Shoreham, from where he escaped to the Continent aboard the coal brig *Surprise*.

Local folklore has it that the King and Lady Jane were stopped and questioned by Parliamentarian soldiers, from which is derived an old nursery rhyme-cum-game as follows:

Q. What's your name?   A. Lady Jane.
Q. Where do you live?   A. Down the lane.
Q. What's your number?   A. Cucumber, etc.

The pair on horseback in the foreground of the picture are thought to be Charles II and Lady Jane Lane, the king minus his Stuart beard and his long hair cropped for disguise. His face was said to have been stained with walnut oil to darken his skin. (Author)

Another historic event witnessed by these ancient walls was when the persecutors of the Revd John Wesley arrived with their captive on the evening of 20 October 1743, intent on having him prosecuted by Justice Lane during the infamous Wednesbury anti-Methodist riots (see also page 24).

This astonishing photograph of about 1925 illustrates the sad fate of Bentley Hall, surrounded on all sides by colliery workings. Amazingly, a pit winding wheel and its scaffold have been sited on the lawned approach to the house. The consequence of this undignified subterranean intrusion was the demolition of Bentley Hall in 1929. (Walsall Local History Centre)

The miller's house, standing in Bentley Mill Lane, is pictured here in 1980, when the grounds were being used as a motor salvage yard. A watermill was first mentioned here in a document of 1239. (Author)

Another view of the mill house, Bentley, showing its architecture to date from about 1840 or earlier. In recent years out of town developments have sprung up along Bentley Mill Lane, as it is in close proximity to junction 10 of the M6. The mill house was torn down in the early 1990s and has been replaced by a fast food restaurant. (Author)

A No. 29 Walsall to Wolverhampton trolleybus crosses County Bridge over the Bentley Canal along Wolverhampton Road, 4 October 1965. The Bentley Canal was opened in 1843 and abandoned in 1961. Today it has been filled in to create a walkway. (The late J.C. Brown)

Bentley Estate shops, 1969. The large Bentley housing estate was mainly laid out in the 1950s with additions in the 1960s and '70s. Most of its residents hail from Darlaston and retain a strong affection for the place. The shops, situated at the junction of Queen Elizabeth Avenue and Cunningham Road, have given their window displays over to steel security shutters out of trading hours. (Stan Hill)

Pictured in 1969, these prefabricated bungalows dated from just after the Second World War, when they provided much-needed housing on a shoestring budget. These properties situated in Cumberland Avenue have now been replaced by modern flats. (Stan Hill)

Two trolleybuses head towards Walsall along Wolverhampton Road, passing the Queen Elizabeth Avenue entrance to the Bentley housing estate, 10 October 1965. The barber's pole, on the right, belongs to a row of long-established shops approached by the service road visible in the foreground. (The late J.C. Brown)

The annual 'witness parade' of mixed Bentley churches is seen passing through Wilkes Avenue, 1960. This would have included the congregations of Bentley Methodist, Emmanuel and St Andrew's churches. (*Walsall Observer*)

Speeches are read at the opening of a St Andrew's church fête at Rubery Owen sportsground in Bentley Road, 1950s. This is now the site of Bentley Leisure Pavilion, operated by Walsall Metropolitan Borough Council. (St Andrew's Church)

The widow of Alfred Ernest Owen, Mrs Florence Lucy Beech Owen, takes to the microphone (right) to declare St Andrew's first garden party open, 1952. This was held at the Wolverhampton Road West home of Mrs Knights, seen standing in the doorway. To the left stands the Revd Desmond Spackman. (St Andrew's Church)

Old St Andrew's Church, Bentley, *c.* 1950. (St Andrew's Church)

The altar of old St Andrew's, *c.* 1950. No attempt was made to disguise the prefabricated method of construction. (St Andrew's Church)

In this unusual and delightful picture, the pews have been taken outside St Andrew's for a spring clean. Florence Jones stands second left in this 1950s study. (St Andrew's Church)

Members of St Andrew's vestry assemble for the camera, 1956. Back row, left to right: George Jones, George Butler, Arthur Monks, Reg Neville, W. Titley, Joe Nicholls, Jim Rolfe, Claude Tennyson. Front row: Mrs I. Tonks, Beatrice Edmonds, the Revd Percy Edmonds, Mrs E.M. Smith. (St Andrew's Church)

A fundraising banner for the new church is just visible above this 1957 picture of St Andrew's youngsters in front of the old church. The Revd Percy Edmonds can be seen standing at the entrance to the right. (St Andrew's Church)

The last anniversary service in St Andrew's old church was held in June 1957. Judging by the cramped conditions it must have been cosy in the winter yet uncomfortable during the summer. (St Andrew's Church)

St Andrew's new church nears completion in the summer of 1957. The foundation stone was laid by the Right Revd G.W. Forbes, Bishop of Lichfield, on 17 November 1956. The land in the foreground is now the entrance to Churchill Road. (St Andrew's Church)

Members of St Andrew's congregation give the church its first lick of paint in preparation for the consecration service in 1957.
(St Andrew's Church)

(Ladies from Bentley Methodist chapel enter a bonnet parade as part of the Queen Elizabeth II silver jubilee celebrations, 27 July 1977. Left to right: Mrs J. Smith, -?-, Lilian Harper, Laura Vaill, Mrs Venvil, Mary Davies. (Marjorie Stockham)

Bentley residents board their float for Darlaston carnival, 1979. Left to right: Marion Higgs, Julie Higgs, Linda Morris, John Morris, Neil Morris, Jenny Wilkinson, Stephen Wilkinson, Paul Wilkinson. (Linda Morris)

4

Darlastonians

What gives a place an identity is its people, and Darlastonians show an affection and pride for their town unequalled anywhere. Darlaston Salavation Army band is pictured here in 1919. (Author)

Councillor Joseph Yardley JP was born at Darlaston in 1848, where a street is named in his memory. A brewer and keen politician, he served the Darlaston Local Board for twelve years before being elected first chairman of Darlaston Urban District Council in 1894. (Author)

John Garrington (1802–77) was the founder of the company that carried his name manufacturing all kinds of iron stampings. After his death, the firm was carried on by his sons Richard and Benjamin, who established the Albert Works at The Green in 1879. (The late Reg Garrington)

Bearded 'Old Father Time', Harold Griffiths, lines up with the clock fairies following a theatrical sketch at Darlaston Town Hall, New Year's Day, 1930. Ivan Harrison is on the far left, while Marie Griffiths plays the 1 o'clock fairy at the centre of the group. (Marie Webster)

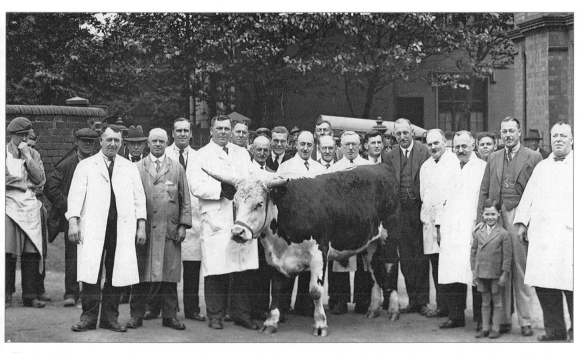

Officials of the 1932 Darlaston carnival pose outside the Town Hall with the unfortunate beast selected for the ox roast. (Author)

This late 1950s Miss Darlaston competition was rounded off with the selection of a senior King and Queen. The lady second from right is Dorothy Purcell, one-time Mayor of Walsall, whose name is given to a school in Bull Lane, Moxley. (John Allen)

Darlaston butchers Edith and Jack Allen supervise the pig roast during the 1953 town carnival. They ran their business from 69 Pinfold Street. (John Allen)

Carnival capers, 1979. Revellers are pictured in Richards Street getting into the swinging '60s mood ready for the grand parade. (*Express & Star*)

An unknown group proudly pose with their winning shield, *c.* 1927. The shield is inscribed: 'Search the Scriptures, Primitive Methodist Connexion, West Midlands District Sunday School Union, Scripture Examination Honour Shield', and was presented by Richard Bayley Esq. of Darlaston in 1915. (Author)

The Revd T.E. Hamer is pictured 175 ft up in front of the new spire of St Lawrence's church in August 1906. Originally from Lancashire, he was appointed rector of Darlaston in 1890. (Author)

Members of St Lawrence's male choir in the churchyard, 1920. Front row, left to right: -?-, -?-, -?-, -?-, Horace Hingley, David Hingley, Sid Joyner, Frank Jones, -?-, Sid Griffiths junior, -?-, -?-. Second row: Charlie Pallet, Arthur Hingley, Jack Gibbons, -?-, Benny Mainwood, Albert Joyner, Herbert Foster, Jack Bedworth, Freddie Humpage, -?-, Eric Cash. Third row: Albert Butler, Jack Smith, -?-, Jabez Howell, Tom Croft, -?-, Sid Griffiths, William Whitehouse (choirmaster). Back row: G. Blakemore, Vic Partridge, ? Robinson, ? Robinson, Arthur Shaw, -?-, Joe Gibbons. (Arthur Hingley)

Methodists from Pinfold Street chapel's young men's Sunday afternoon Bible class outside the chapel, *c.* 1910. (Marjorie Stockham)

Ladies from Pinfold Street Methodists 'ladies own' group on a coach outing, 1930s. The tour operator, Mason's, still runs excursions from the town. Chapel caretaker Mrs Hunt is on the extreme left. (Marjorie Stockham)

Guest, Keen and Nettlefold's bowling team with a district trophy, 1952. Otherwise known as GKN, the firm which produced industrial fastenings had its sports ground in Hall Street, now the home of Darlaston Community Association Sports and Social Centre. (John Farquhar)

Woods Bank Prims FC line up for a 1920/21 season official photograph. Woods Bank is an area between Moxley and Darlaston. (Noreen Hunt)

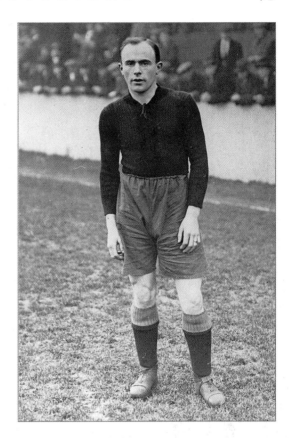

Footballer Leonard Rhodes, who lived at 63 Wolverhampton Street, signed to play for Darlaston Town FC on 22 July 1925 for an agreed sum of £2 per week. The football ground still exists at its original site just off Waverley Road. (Eric Woolley)

Winners of the Beddow Memorial Cup in 1953 were Darlaston Amateurs, pictured here with the trophy. (St Andrew's Church)

Cricketers from Pinfold Street Methodist chapel at an unknown ground, *c.* 1900. (Marjorie Stockham)

Guest, Keen and Nettlefold's cricket team at the company sports field in Hall Street, mid-1950s. St. Lawrence church spire can just be seen in the background. (John Farquhar)

Wardens from 'C' group of Darlaston Civil Defence contingent, June 1943. (Jack K. Aston)

The cadets of Darlaston Air Training Corps at Newton air base, Nottinghamshire, 1945. (Horace Page)

No. 13 platoon, 23 commando of the 37 battalion of South Staffordshire Home Guard at Darlaston, *c.* 1940. Back row, left to right: -?-, -?-, ? Gainsborough, -?-, A. Marston, ? Dunkley. Third row: H. Rayson, ? Slim, -?-, ? Yates, J. Hough, ? Corns, -?-, -?-, J. Fellows. Second row: H. Shaw, -?-, Sergeant N. Linton, Lieutenant Hutchinson, -?-, C. Perks, Corporal T. Day. Front row: -?-, -?-, H. Winsper, -?-. (Irene Fellows)

No. 3 platoon of the above-mentioned battalion, *c.* 1940. All these men worked in Rubery Owen's structural department. (Doreen Horton)

Darlaston Home Guard headquarters platoon at Charles Richards sports ground, now the site of Bowling Green Close, 1943. Back row, left to right: -?-, Corporal Gibb, Sergeant Staite, Sergeant Stokes, -?-, -?-. Front row: Lieutenant Kingston, -?-, -?-, Sergeant Major Cumpsie, Captain Walker, Lieutenant Harrison, -?-, -?-, Sergeant Roberts. (Alfred Staite)

Rubery Owen Home Guard outside the works canteen and, to the right, the drill hall in Queen Street, 1943. The canteen building is now demolished but the drill hall – later the personnel department – still survives. (Arthur Hingley)

Residents from the Rough Hay housing estate gather at the Rough Hay Tavern, Rough Hay Road, to celebrate VE Day. Seated second from the left with arms folded is the licensee Jack Perry, whose fiery temper earned him the nickname 'the mad-un'! Another local character fondly remembered is William Walters, known around Darlaston

as 'Billy Muggins'. He can be seen standing on the far left of the back row. Billy earned his living by repairing discarded hardware and selling it on again. This was augmented by playing his mouth organ around the local public houses, cap in hand. (Mick Horton)

Before he commenced in business as a cycle dealer (see page 92), Len Mitchell was a pianist for the silent movies and was also the piano tuner for schools in the Darlaston district. Here he is pictured standing to the left of the pay booth at the Picturedrome, Crescent Road, in 1925, whilst promoting the film *In a Monastery Garden*. (Marion Evans)

Members of Slater Street Methodist chapel amateur dramatics group take to the stage for a 1930s production. Second left is Hilda Hopkins (née Lewis). (Joyce O'Connor)

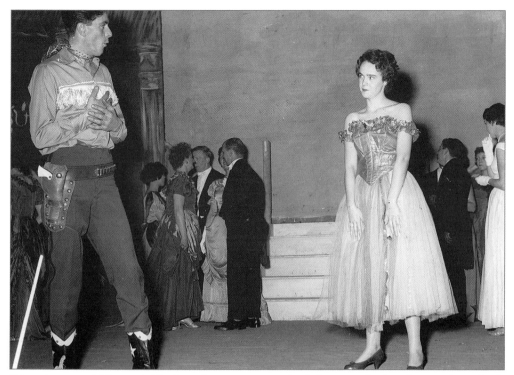

Brian Amos and Margaret Hingley take centre stage in St Lawrence's church operatic society's production of *Annie Get Your Gun*, staged in about 1960. (Margaret Dainty)

The young thespian on the right playing the 'pipes of Pan' is the popular actress Sue Nicholls, today famed for her role as Audrey Roberts in *Coronation Street*. The daughter of the late Lord Harmar Nicholls, she was born in 1943 and spent her early childhood in the district of Pleck near Darlaston, from where she would often visit her grandparents' public house, the White Lion in King Street (see page 24). The play was performed on parents' day at Woodland Grange school in nearby Wednesbury, *c.* 1949. In Greek mythology Pan is a goat-man, the protector of animals, who plays on a flute of reeds. (Sue Nicholls)

Pinfold Street school netball team during the 1951/2 playing season. Back row, left to right: Marion Fiddler, Valerie Malsbury, Gillian Folls, Irene Brookes, Sheila Hurley. Front row: Anthea Wearing, Pat Thompson, Pauline Davies, Gladys Randall. (Valerie Allen)

Teacher Mr Scarth joins pupils from Pinfold Street juniors for this school photograph, *c.* 1951. (Valerie Allen)

Old Church girls juniors are pictured at their aptly named School Street premises, 1959. (Arthur Hingley)

Physical education teacher Mr Williams in the centre of the second row in this group picture of Slater Street secondary modern boys, 1950. (Mick Horton)

Salisbury Street secondary modern girls with teacher Mr Wilkins, centre, 1953. (Arthur Hingley)

Members of Slater Street Methodist youth club gather for this mid-1950s photograph. (Arthur Hingley)

Mrs Edith Allen (right) presents a gardening trophy during a civic awards presentation evening, *c.* 1960. (John Allen)

Garrington's staff on a works outing, *c.* 1900. Sixth from right in a straw hat is Bert Garrington. He was the grandson of founder John Garrington, and sold the company to Guest, Keen and Nettlefold's in 1918. (The late Reg Garrington)

Guest, Keen and Nettlefold's staff gather outside the factory, late 1940s. (John Farquhar)

Senior staff from Wilkins and Mitchell power press plant enjoy a pint following a long service presentation awards evening, 1973. Seated, left to right: Len Greatrex, Charles Moore, Ray Fowndes, Joseph Albert Fellows, Jack Hickman. (Irene Fellows)

W. Martin Winn employees don sailors' uniforms for this patriotic parade of the mid-1930s (see also title page). The company, which produced nuts and bolts, was situated in Kendricks Road. (David Robinson)

W. Martin Winn ladies assemble in the office grounds, *c.* 1947. Back row, left to right: M. Russell, M. Smith, N. Stringer, H. Jervis, M. Walters, S. Wallace, M. Wilkes. Third row: M. Riley, O. Owen. Second row: O. Hays, E. Marson, E. Cattell, B. Allen, J. Huffadine, F. Belcher. Front row: D. George, J. Perry, T. Garrington, O. Pattison. (Mary Yeomans)

Dorsett Road residents gather for an informal photograph, *c.* 1952. (John Farquhar)

This garden party was held to celebrate the coronation of Queen Elizabeth II, 2 June 1953. (Ned Williams)

Sir Alfred Owen, one of the sons of co-founder of the Rubery Owen empire, Alfred Ernest Owen, celebrates the coronation with Darlaston youngsters, 2 June 1953. (Black Country Living Museum)

Another coronation party commences, 2 June 1953, this time at Fallings Heath chapel. (Black Country Living Museum)

Darlaston acrobats Leo Phillips and Jack Butler are pictured performing an act called 'The Awakening' under their stage names of Leo Brampton and Jack Roland. Along with Leo's father, Maurice, they travelled the world billed as the 'Omega Trio' performing strongman stunts. Before Darlaston's first cinema opened in 1911, Leo Phillips used to put on film shows for 1d admission. (June Taylor)

Regulars from The Fountain public house, Walsall Road, are snapped on a coach outing in 1953. Harry Yarnall is on the far right, ready to play the accordion. (Harry Yarnall)

5

Kings Hill

Kings Hill is a mixed residential and industrial district situated between two main roads running parallel from Wednesbury to Darlaston, Old Park Road and Darlaston Road. The latter is shown here in about 1920. (National Tramway Museum)

Old Park Road residents pose for the cameraman, 1906. In the distance is Kings Hill Board School, built in 1887. The houses have been replaced with Kings Hill telephone exchange. (Author)

Mrs Lucy Phillips stands at the gateway to her Old Park Road home, 1908. This appears to be the house on the left of the picture above. (Noreen Hunt)

Kings Hill school pupils, 1888. See if you can find the set of twin boys! (Ecce Scott)

Ivy Johnson conducts the 'orchestra' in this delightful 1930s study taken at Kings Hill school. The young musicians are as follows. Back row, left to right: Marion Mitchell, -?-, -?-, -?-, -?-, Dorothy Mitchell. Third row: -?-, Jean Bailey, Christine Holland, Doreen Cooper, -?-. Second row: Beryl Humphries, ? Greatrex, Kathleen Goode, -?-. Front row: Joseph Stubbs, -?-, -?-, -?-, Geoff Tinsley, -?-, Charlie Simms. (Marion Evans)

Earmarked for demolition, Kings Hill Board School was destroyed in this fierce blaze in 1992. The caretaker's house situated in Joynson Street still survives, as does the secondary modern school building seen in the background along Old Park Road. (Author)

Cycle dealer Len Mitchell established his business in a shed erected in the garden of his home on the corner of the Old Park Road and Franchise Street. His twin daughters, Dorothy and Marion (on tricycle), are pictured outside the original premises in 1928. The girls – who only had to cross the road to school – appear with the school 'orchestra' on the previous page. (Marion Evans)

Security of Len Mitchell's wooden building was poor, so after repeated thefts it was decided to move the business into the front room of the family home, 62 Old Park Road. The building has now reverted to residential use and today is re-numbered 136 Old Park Road. (Marion Evans)

Hill Street, seen here in July 1965, runs between Old Park Road and Walsall Road. Many of the old terraced houses have now been demolished. (Bernard Minton)

Local boys enjoy a game of football at Kings Hill Park, 1950. The park was opened in 1900 on the site of a colliery mound. (Author)

Kings Hill post office has little changed since being photographed in 1950. The property to the right, however, 201 Darlaston Road, has now been demolished. (Author)

Built between the two world wars, Kings Hill Tavern stood on the corner of Darlaston Road and Woden Road West until demolition in the 1990s. (Alan John)

Rubery Owen's Kings Hill branch works ran from Forge Street towards Wednesbury, occupying a considerable length of Darlaston Road. A modern industrial estate now stands on the site. (Freda Riley)

Production workers head home through the factory gates at the end of another shift at Wilkins and Mitchell's domestic appliance plant, where the famous Servis brand of washing machines was manufactured. Cars were still a luxury for many in 1966 when this photograph was taken, evident by the lack of congestion along Darlaston

Road. Instead, bicycle sheds were always full. The spire of St Lawrence's Church can be seen on the horizon.
(Darlaston Rotary Club)

Young members of Joynson Street centenary chapel front this 1937 gathering of the congregation. (Horace Page)

Joint meetings of Slater Street and Joynson Street Methodist youth clubs were held in the Sunday school to the rear of the Kings Hill chapel during the Second World War. The Revd Mr Agg is seated at the centre of the front row in this 1943 picture of the extended gathering. Right of him are sister Claire Powers and youth club chairman Geoff Tinsley. (Geoff Tinsley)

6

Darlaston Inside Out

The loss of self-governing status and recent decline in industry, together with the removal of once-familiar buildings, have collectively brought about great physical and social changes in Darlaston, witnessed over the last three decades and beyond. Here, the last chairman of Darlaston Urban District Council, Mrs Elizabeth Ellen Wilkinson JP, presides over a committee meeting in the council chamber of the town hall early in 1966. Since this date Darlaston has been governed by its larger neighbour, Walsall. The ashtrays made at George Ward (Moxley) Limited were inscribed 'Made in Darlaston – of Darlaston'. (Darlaston Rotary Club)

Old Darlaston swimming baths, 1969. The Victoria Road pool was opened in 1938 by the Earl of Harrowby. (Stan Hill)

The interior of the old baths, 1966. The building closed to the public in 1993 and was later demolished. A new pool has been constructed on the site and will be in full use by 2001. (Darlaston Rotary Club)

Junior members of Pinfold Street Methodist chapel prepare to stage a nativity play in 1946. (Marjorie Stockham)

Pinfold Street chapel, *c.* 1920. Built in 1810, it was later enlarged and modified – but has now been demolished. Some graves still remain amongst the Wesley's Fold housing development which occupies the former burial ground. (Marjorie Stockham)

Slater Street Methodist chapel was opened in 1910 as a replacement for a chapel in nearby Bell Street, which closed in 1908. The original chapel with its tower and spire was demolished in 1979. The Sunday school, seen to the left, is still in use. (Black Country Living Museum)

The lofty interior of Slater Street chapel, *c.* 1930. (Joyce O'Connor)

St George's church was built in the Early English style on land between Bush Street and The Green, and was consecrated in 1852. (Author)

An exterior view of St George's church, 1968. The church was demolished in 1975 leaving only a sculpture of St George and the dragon on the site, dedicated to the memory of Councillor George John Garrington JP in 1959. (Alan Price)

Bull Street looking in the direction of St Lawrence's Church and the post office, *c.* 1915. A horse and cart cross the railway bridge at a spot known locally as Bull Piece, which gives access to Victoria Road. Out of sight in the cutting, between 1863 and 1889, stood Darlaston Town railway station. (Author)

Horse-drawn traffic passes either side of a tram along Darlaston Road looking in the direction of Wednesbury, *c.* 1913. The house far right is today the premises of a printer. Adjacent posters advertise rival cinemas, the Olympic and the Picturedrome. (National Tramway Museum)

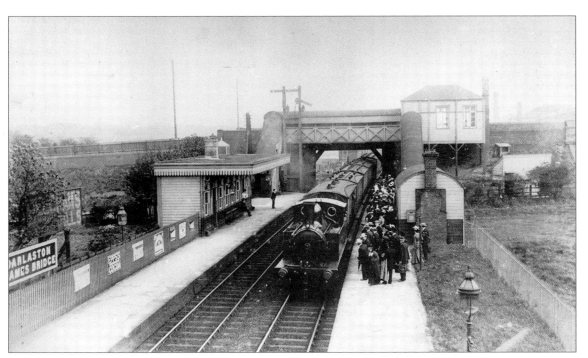

James Bridge railway station was opened in 1837 as a halt on the Grand Junction Railway, connecting Birmingham with Warrington. Here, a steam train pulls in, *c.* 1906. (Eric Woolley)

Coal merchant Charles Simmonds' cart is transformed into a carnival float with the theme James Bridge Harem, *c.* 1925. James Bridge is an area midway between Darlaston and Walsall and takes its name from a crossing over the river Tame. Note the mis-spelled banner. (Author)

Cramp Hill near its intersection with Cross Street, April 1959. (Stan Hill)

Alma Street in October 1963, prior to development which saw the construction of Alma Court multi-storey flats. Today these in turn await demolition. (Stan Hill)

School Street, which is reached from Alma Street, October 1963. Its old houses were also demolished to make way for Alma Court and the neighbouring Leys Court. (Stan Hill)

Eldon Street has been wiped off the Darlaston streetscape since this photograph was taken in October 1963. It ran between Bilston Street and Little Cross Street, where its name has been adopted by a short private road. (Stan Hill)

Class II of Dorsett Road school break from lessons for this photograph on 7 October 1920, as is evident from the information on the blackboard. All pupils sit with their arms at their sides to prevent fidgeting. (Author)

This rare picture shows the interior of All Saints' church, which was built in Walsall Road in 1872 and destroyed by an enemy bomb on 31 July 1942. A new church was consecrated in 1952. (Marjorie Stockham)

A children's Christmas party is held in the foyer of the Olympic cinema in the early 1950s. Affectionately known as the 'Limp', the picture house which stood on the corner of Blockall and Bell Street was opened in 1912 and closed in 1956. (Arthur Hingley)

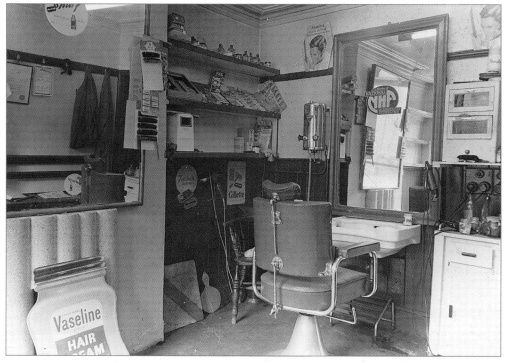

The interior of W.E. Cownley's shaving saloon, Pinfold Street, during the 1950s, when hair creams were much used in gents' hairstyling. The business continues to thrive today in its original premises. (W.E. Cownley)

The residential end of High Street, 1971, following the removal of its northern side to allow construction of The Leys traffic island. Since then the last house seen to the right and the adjoining Seven Stars public house have been demolished to improve access to Willenhall Street. Recently the addresses of the remaining buildings have been incorporated into King Edward Street. (Alan Price)

New Street properties, April 1959. All these buildings have been replaced by modern housing. The spire of St Lawrence's church rises above the chimneypots. (Stan Hill)

Heath Road properties from the junction of Station Street, June 1962. Modern housing now replaces the old terraces pictured here. (Stan Hill)

Heath Road is one of Darlaston's longest roads, linking Fallings Heath to The Green. At its junction with Richards Street stood Fletcher's corner shop, seen here in about 1955. Note the vending machines fixed to the wall. (Black Country Living Museum)

Albert Street residents Minnie and Bert Hopkins with their daughter, also Minnie, at the rear of their home, 1931. Albert Street was cleared in 1970 and replaced with open-plan housing. (Joyce O'Connor)

Bull Street, April 1959. To the left a gap in the building line marks the entrance to Albert Street. The public house to the right of this junction was the Cottage of Content, today the premises of a sportswear manufacturer. (Stan Hill)

Blockall was the main link between The Green and Darlaston town centre before the opening of St Lawrence Way in 1971. This 1968 picture shows Fosbrook's outfitters who traded from 22–23 Blockall, specialising in school uniforms. (Alan Price)

Blockall's junction with Addenbrooke Street, 1968. The Mission of the Good Shepherd church, built in 1890, stands on the left. The properties to the right of the junction are part of The Green. (Alan Price)

Women factory workers from Wiley's nuts and bolts take a break from work, 1927. Foreman Ben Wilkes is third from right at the back. Iron rods for bolt-making are stacked against the factory walls. (Arthur Hingley)

Latch manufacturers Yardley and Carter's Willenhall Street premises, *c.* 1910. The horse is harnessed ready for a delivery run. Again, iron rods (left) are an essential commodity. (Author)

The stamp shop of Garrington's Albert works at The Green, *c.* 1900. The unguarded machine belt seen to the right would not be allowed today. (The late Reg Garrington)

The original offices to Garrington's Albert works, *c.* 1900. The double gates gave access to the Garrington family home, Albert House. Note the bust of Prince Albert above the office door. (The late Reg Garrington)

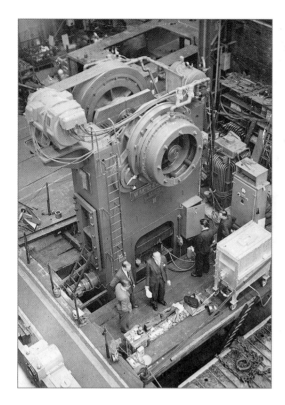

Prospective German customers examining a blanking press at Wilkins and Mitchell's power press plant, 1954. The press operatives on the right are Ray Fowndes and Joseph Albert Fellows. (Irene Fellows)

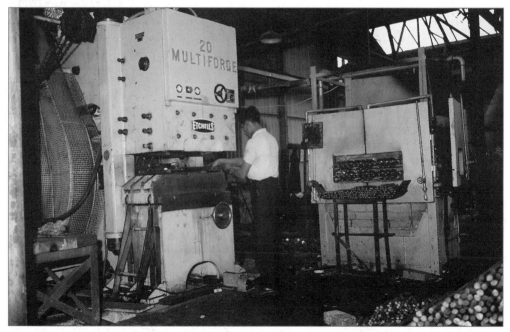

David Etchells Limited produced nut and bolt manufacturing machines at Bull Piece and later their Stafford Road factory, supplying not only Darlaston but the world. Here, an Etchells multi-forge is being operated at a local factory in 1966. (Darlaston Rotary Club)

Operatives at Rubery Owen & Company assemble 'Bowser Impactor' petrol pumps, 1966. The Bowser organisation was established in the USA in 1905 and became associated with Rubery Owen in 1952, before being totally acquired by the Darlaston firm in 1963. (Darlaston Rotary Club)

Comrade Cycles operated from the Alma Works situated between Alma Street and Stafford Road. This 1966 picture shows the frame shop. Today the Hotel Petite stands on the site. (Darlaston Rotary Club)

This picture of the huge Atlas nut and bolt works appears to have been taken on a day off in 1966. The works situated between Station Street, Bills Street and Salisbury Street were the largest of Darlaston's nut and bolt factories, operated by the firm of Guest, Keen and Nettlefold. (Darlaston Rotary Club)

Trainee nut and bolt production workers learn their trade, at Guest, Keen and Nettlefold's Atlas works in 1966. (Darlaston Rotary Club)

Women operatives keep a watchful eye over bolt threading machines, 1966. There are no seats to relieve aching backs and legs. Note the broom and shovel to the right, essential for clearing the build-up of waste thread around the machinery. (Darlaston Rotary Club)

Established in 1879, F.H. Lloyd steelworks' main entrance was decorated to celebrate the coronation of Queen Elizabeth II, 2 June 1953. The 36-acre site straddled the border between Wednesbury and Darlaston at James Bridge. Note the works clock. (Black Country Living Museum)

Castings being produced at F.H. Lloyd in 1966. On the far left a foundry worker turns the steering wheel which tilts the giant container of molten steel, allowing it to pour. A colleague collects the white-hot liquid in a crucible ready to pour into the moulds at his side. (Darlaston Rotary Club)

Pictured in about 1950, George Rose Park, Wolverhampton Street, was opened on 1 November 1924, taking its name from its instigator, Councillor John George Rose, who sadly died before its completion. In the distance to the right of the bandstand can be seen a pump house and chimney belonging to the nearby Walsall Canal. (Author)

The bandstand at George Rose Park, 1963. Today only the brick base remains where locals were once serenaded. (Author)

The Bradford Arms was better known to locals as the Frying Pan. Stories differ as to how it acquired this name. The pub, which stood on the corner of Bilston Street and Eldon Street, is seen here in 1968. (Alan Price)

Eldon Street had been swept away by the mid-1970s, leaving the Bradford Arms marooned next to the new St Lawrence Way. Later it was replaced by a new public house officially named the Frying Pan. (Terry Price)

The Dog and Pheasant, Blockall, 7 September 1968. This was demolished in 1970 to make room for St Lawrence Way. (Alan Price)

Another Blockall watering hole was the Scott Arms, which stood on the corner of Foster Street. It was photographed on 7 September 1968. (Alan Price)

The Engine Inn, Bell Street, 7 September 1968. Public houses seem to defy the bulldozer for some time after neighbouring properties disappear. (Alan Price)

The corner of Dangerfield Lane and Moxley Road was the location of the Duke of York, seen here on 10 August 1964. A no. 7 trolleybus heads towards Darlaston town centre on a stretch of road that is now a dual carriageway. All the buildings on the left have been demolished, with a rest home replacing the Duke of York. (The late J.C. Brown)

Members of W. Martin Winn works tennis club line up for the camera in 1922. Seated second from right is Lydia Morris (née Morgan). The Station Works were so named because of their close proximity to James Bridge railway station. Winn's produced nuts and bolts as well as bright drawn steel for the trade. (Chas Morris)

Local children assemble on a float decked up by the Free Gardeners Friendly Society outside their King Edward Street premises, to celebrate the silver jubilee of King George V and Queen Mary, 6 May 1935. (Mary Yeomans)

The junction of Moxley Road, Pinfold Street and Dangerfield Lane, 1963. The houses behind the trolleybus are today incorporated into Pinfold Street, but were once known as Pinfold Alley and later still St John's Road. The locals, however, christened it 'Shitten Alley'! (The late J.C. Brown)

Pictured here on 16 November 1963, the Staffordshire Knot public house still stands on the corner of Wolverhampton Street and Pinfold Street today, although the adjoining property and those opposite have been removed along with the traffic island. This part of Darlaston is anciently known as Catherine's Cross. (The late J.C. Brown)

ACKNOWLEDGEMENTS

The author would like to express his sincere thanks to the following people for either the loan of photographs or their kind assistance:

All Saints' Moxley Parish Church Council, John Allen, Valerie Allen, Jack K. Aston, the Black Country Living Museum, the late J.C. Brown, W.E. Cownley, Margaret Dainty, Darlaston Rotary Club, Alan Davies, Katharine Dudley, Jan Endean, Marion Evans, *Express & Star*, John Farquhar, Irene Fellows, the late Reg Garrington, Jack Gittings, Stan Hill, Arthur Hingley, Doreen Horton, Mick Horton, John Hughes, the Revd Paul Hunt of St Andrew's Church, Bentley, Noreen Hunt, Alan John, Jayne Marsh, Midland United Newspapers, Bernard Minton, Chas Morris, Linda Morris, National Tramway Museum, Sue Nicholls, Jim Oakley, Joyce O'Connor, Jim Owen, Horace Page, David Phillips, Jean Phillips, Alan Price, Terry Price, Freda Riley, David Robinson, Kate Robinson, Ecce Scott, Gillian Sedgwick, Gwen Sedgwick, Terry Smitheman, Alfred Staite, Sam Stevenson, Marjorie Stockham, Olive Swift, June Taylor, Geoff Tinsley, Walsall Local History Centre, *Walsall Observer*, Marie Webster, Cynthia Wilkes, Ned Williams, Glynn Wilton, Harry Yarnall, Mary Yeomans.

Licensee Patrick McCormack stands third from the right with regulars and their offspring outside the Barrel Inn, Horton Street, *c.* 1900. The building survives today, converted to residential use. (Mary Yeomans)